The Little Book of

BAD MOODS

WRITTEN BY LOTTA SONNINEN

ILLUSTRATIONS BY PIIA AHO

GALLERY BOOKS

New York   London   Toronto   Sydney   New Delhi

Gallery Books
An Imprint of Simon & Schuster, Inc.
1230 Avenue of the Americas
New York, NY 10020

First Gallery Books hardcover edition February 2019

GALLERY BOOKS and colophon are registered trademarks of Simon & Schuster, Inc.

For information about special discounts for bulk purchases, please contact Simon & Schuster Special Sales at 1-866-506-1949 or business@simonandschuster.com.

The Simon & Schuster Speakers Bureau can bring authors to your live event. For more information or to book an event, contact the Simon & Schuster Speakers Bureau at 1-866-248-3049 or visit our website at www.simonspeakers.com.

Manufactured in the United States of America

10 9 8 7 6 5 4 3 2 1

Library of Congress Cataloging-in-Publication Data is available.

ISBN 978-1-9821-2262-1

Contents

_ _ _ _ _ _

BLAME
OTHERS

List what's wrong with your spouse.

✗
....

✗
....

✗
....

✗
....

✗
....

List what's wrong with your parents.

✗
....

✗
....

✗
....

✗
....

✗
....

✗
....

List what's wrong with your kids.

X _____

X _____

X _____

X _____

X _____

List what's wrong with your boss.

X _____

X _____

X _____

X _____

X _____

X _____

List what's wrong with your friends.

NAME	FAULTS

What former boss/colleague/employee
of yours still makes you angry and why?

Which of your EXes do you still hate
and why?

How do you spot an idiot **in the checkout line**?

How do you spot an idiot *walking down the street*?

How do you spot an idiot **IN A RESTAURANT**?

How do you spot an idiot **on a date**?

How do you spot an idiot
IN TRAFFIC?

How do you spot an idiot TRAVELING
ABROAD?

How do you spot an idiot online?

How do you spot an idiot AT WORK?

Idiots I've met *at work*:

_____

_____

_____

_____

Idiots I've met IN TRAFFIC:

_____

_____

_____

_____

IDIOTS I'VE MET *on dates*:

_____

_____

_____

_____

Idiots I've met **at bars**:

Idiots I've met **THROUGH MY HOBBIES**:

Idiots I've met **online**:

List acquaintances or celebrities who...

...have had it way too easy

✗

✗

✗

✗

...think too much of themselves

✗

✗

✗

✗

...have no idea what's best for them

✗

✗

✗

✗

...should just go back to school

×

×

×

×

...should think more before opening their mouths

×

×

×

×

The absolutely most annoying type of person is

Your boss's most irritating habit

_____

_____

_____

Your spouse's most irritating habit

_____

_____

_____

Your teacher's most irritating habit

_____

_____

_____

Your child's most irritating habit

_____

_____

_____

Your grandmother's most irritating habit

_____

_____

_____

Your neighbor's most irritating habit

_____

_____

_____

The most irritating thing about TV

_____

_____

_____

The most irritating thing about politics

_____

_____

_____

NAME

NAMES

What's wrong with your life?

WHAT'S WRONG

WHOSE FAULT IS IT?

Make a list of people who are **less talented than you** but still *more successful.*

X

X

X

X

X

X
X

X

X

X

X

I'M JEALOUS OF...

NAME

REASON

DRAW

THE LINE

Give this **voodoo doll** a face or
other distinguishing features.

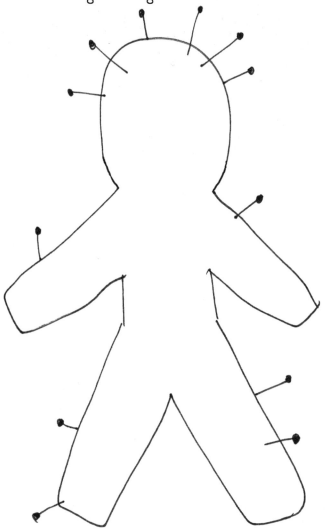

Draw an U G L Y animal.

Draw and color
AN UGLY OUTFIT.

Draw and color
DISGUSTING FOOD.

Draw **a traffic sign**
that would forbid something you hate.

Design some **ugly** wallpaper.

CHANNEL YOUR BITTERNESS

Think of three ways to irritate
YOUR SPOUSE.

-

-

-

Think of three ways to irritate
YOUR PARENTS.

-

-

-

Think of three ways to irritate
YOUR COWORKERS.

-

-

-

Think of three ways to irritate
YOUR BOSS.

-

-

-

Think of three ways to irritate
YOUR FELLOW TRAVELERS.

-

-

-

Think of three ways to be irritating
ONLINE.

-

-

-

Fill in the blanks.

My life would be much easier if ....
wasn't so ....

The world would be a much better place if ....
didn't always ....

.... can't even .... ,
and yet he/she always ....

I get bored out of my mind whenever ....
starts to talk about his/her ....

The next time .... starts to .... ,
I'm going to lose it.

I have no idea why I ever .... with ....

I truly don't know why .... was ever invented.

I don't understand why men always have to ....

38

I don't understand why women always have to

_____ .

I don't understand why kids always have to

_____ .

I don't understand why _____ always has to _____ .

It's the 21st century, for heaven's sake. Why do

_____ still _____ ?

If I'd known that _____ , I never would have _____ .

All _____ are idiots because they _____ .

If I could decide, _____

would be forbidden from _____ .

If I could decide, _____ would be

erased from the earth.

39

HOW TO MAKE
ANY DAY
A BAD DAY

List what was wrong with this week.

	I WAS ANNOYED BY	THIS RUINED THE DAY
Monday		
Tuesday		
Wednesday		

	I WAS ANNOYED BY	THIS RUINED THE DAY
Thursday		
Friday		
Saturday		
Sunday		

The Vacation of My
NIGHTMARES

Place:

Company:

Schedule:

Menu:

The Christmas
FROM HELL

Place:

Company:

Schedule:

Menu:

Keep an ingratitude journal!
List everything that bothered you this week.

Monday I was annoyed by...

Tuesday I was annoyed by...

Wednesday I was annoyed by...

Thursday I was annoyed by...

_____

_____

_____

Friday I was annoyed by...

_____

_____

_____

Saturday I was annoyed by...

_____

_____

_____

Sunday I was annoyed by...

_____

_____

_____

LIFE SUCKS

ONLINE

Most infuriating status updates

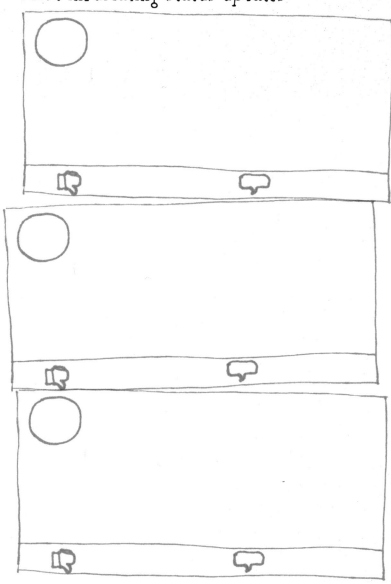

Stupidest blogs

○

○

○

Instacrap

☐

☐

☐

☐

Most birdbrained tweets  %#?!4

 Emojis that need to be punched in the face

worst computer trouble

Most incompetent IT support

Draw new emojis
that express rage or frustration.

Use this space to write emails you wish you could send but won't ever dare.

✕ ➢

Recipient:

CC:

Subject:

Message:

📎 🕒

X

Recipient:
_____

CC:
_____

Subject:
_____

Message:

Recipient:

CC:

Subject:

Message:

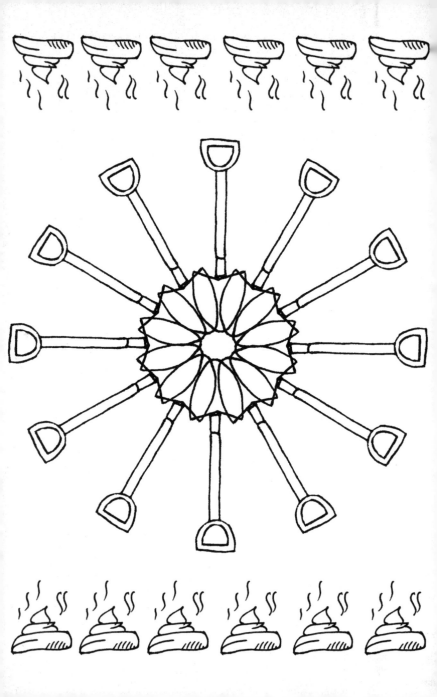

NO FORGETTING

NO
FORGIVING

I most **regret**...

_____

_____

_____

_____

_____

_____

_____

_____

_____

_____

_____

_____

I'll **never** forgive...

I'm STILL bitter about...

_____

_____

_____

_____

_____

_____

_____

_____

_____

_____

_____

_____

_____

List situations where you didn't think of
a **GOOD COMEBACK** until it was over.

TIME, PLACE AND PEOPLE	PERFECT COMEBACK

TIME, PLACE AND PEOPLE | PERFECT COMEBACK

Worst **VACATION DISASTER**

Worst **RELATIONSHIP DISASTER**

Worst *purchase disaster*

Worst HAIR DISASTER

worst **outfit disaster**

....

....

....

worst **party disaster**

....

....

....

worst **COOKING DISASTER**

....

....

worst **CHILDHOOD DISASTER**

....

....

....

worst **school** memory

....

....

....

worst **SCHOOL FOOD** memory

....

....

....

worst personal hygiene memory

....

....

....

worst *doctor's office* memory

....

....

....

worst *dentist visit* memory

---

worst **ONLINE** memory

---

worst **DATE** memory

---

worst **DIY** memory

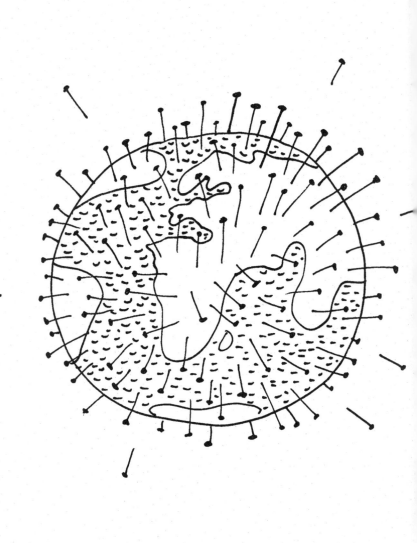

FIND
THE BAD
IN THE
WORLD

What ruins **WORK?**

- -

- -

- -

What ruins a *meal*?

- -

- -

- -

What ruins a **road trip**?

- -

- -

- -

What ruins A BUS RIDE?

- -

- -

- -

what ruins a *flight*?

what ruins a **visit to a restaurant**?

what ruins A MOVIE?

what ruins a **TRIP TO THE SUPERMARKET**?

what ruins a *trip to the doctor*?

--- --- --- --- --- --- --- --- --- --- --- --- --- --- --- --- ---

--- --- --- --- --- --- --- --- --- --- --- --- --- --- --- --- ---

--- --- --- --- --- --- --- --- --- --- --- --- --- --- --- --- ---

what ruins a **NIGHT IN**?

--- --- --- --- --- --- --- --- --- --- --- --- --- --- --- --- ---

--- --- --- --- --- --- --- --- --- --- --- --- --- --- --- --- ---

--- --- --- --- --- --- --- --- --- --- --- --- --- --- --- --- ---

what ruins a TV SHOW?

--- --- --- --- --- --- --- --- --- --- --- --- --- --- --- --- ---

--- --- --- --- --- --- --- --- --- --- --- --- --- --- --- --- ---

--- --- --- --- --- --- --- --- --- --- --- --- --- --- --- --- ---

what ruins a **BOOK**?

--- --- --- --- --- --- --- --- --- --- --- --- --- --- --- --- ---

--- --- --- --- --- --- --- --- --- --- --- --- --- --- --- --- ---

--- --- --- --- --- --- --- --- --- --- --- --- --- --- --- --- ---

What ruins a **FEW DAYS OFF FROM WORK**?

What ruins a *vacation*?

What ruins a **party**?

What ruins a **WORKOUT**?

What's most irritating in **THE CITY**?

_____

_____

_____

What's most irritating in **THE COUNTRY**?

_____

_____

_____

What's most irritating **ABOUT THE GOVERNMENT**?

_____

_____

What's most irritating in **NEWSPAPERS**?

_____

_____

_____

What's most irritating on **TV**?

What's most irritating about **SOCIETY**?

What's the most irritating **LAW**?

What's most annoying about **kids**?

What's most annoying about **TEENAGERS**?

What's most annoying about *adults*?

What's most annoying about **THE ELDERLY**?

What's most annoying about
ANIMALS?

What's most annoying about **you**?

What's most annoying about **this book**?

My least favorite candy is...

My least favorite food is...

My least favorite drink is...

The most pointless tourist attraction is...

The stupidest form of entertainment is...

The worst music is...

The worst chore is...

The dumbest kind of exercise is...

_____

The most ridiculous piece of clothing is...

_____

The most pointless status symbol is...

_____

DRAW SOMETHING STUPID AND POINTLESS

The most pointless invention is...

_____

The most pointless pastime is...

_____

The most pointless profession is...

_____

The most pointless animal is...

_____

The most pointless saying is...

_____

The most pointless conversation topic is...

_____

The biggest waste of money is...

_____

It's gauche to...

It's ridiculous to...

It's childish to...

It's rude to...

It's beyond the pale to...

It's unforgivable to...

It's overrated to...

List all the ACHES and PAINS you've suffered from, suffer from now, or fear you may suffer from in the future.

_____

_____

_____

_____

_____

_____

_____

_____

_____

_____

_____

_____

BADDEN
YOUR
VOCABULARY

IRRITATING, *annoying*, INFURIATING...

Continue the list!

IDIOT, numbskull, _twit..._

Continue the list!

write **swear words** and **insults** in different handwriting.

Why don't you go...

Eat...

write the swear words you know in a foreign language.

write all the swear words you know **in English.**

Which trendy words/phrases do you hate?

_____

_____

_____

What words/phrases make it easy to spot a snob?

_____

_____

_____

Which rude words/phrases do you find most repulsive?

_____

_____

_____

Stupidest old sayings

_____

_____

_____

Words only ever used by

REDNECKS

....

....

....

SNOBS

....

....

....

TEENAGE BRATS

....

....

....

OLD FOSSILS

....

....

....

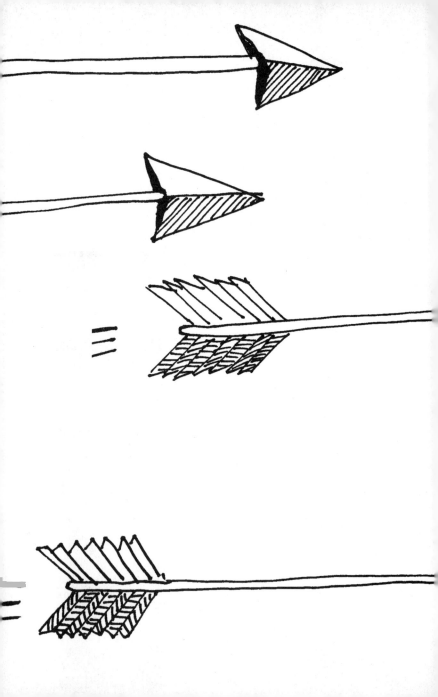

JUST

SAY

IT ALREADY

Most people don't understand these simple things:

Name four people you'd like to
TELL OFF.
USE THE SPEECH
BUBBLES TO GIVE
THEM A PIECE
OF YOUR
MIND.

NAME

NAME

write your irritating neighbor A NASTY NOTE.

Write a message to your former teacher you STILL **HATE**.

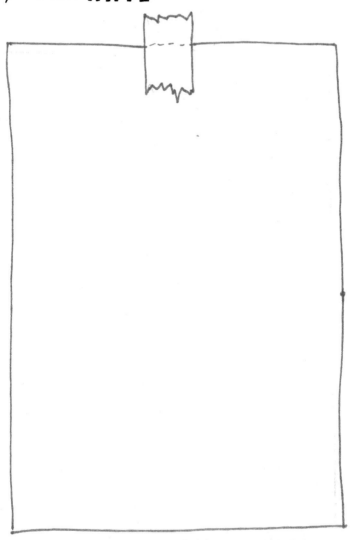

Write a message to a salesperson/waiter/ etc. who insulted you forever ago.

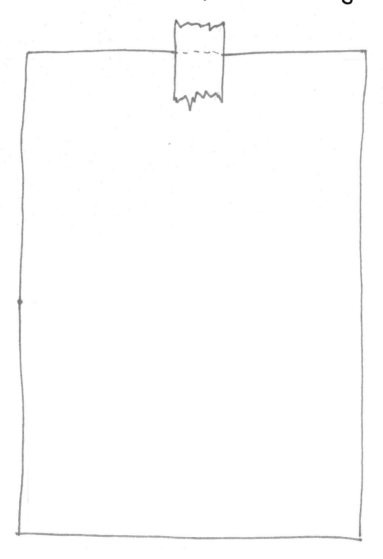

Write a message to your EX you still think is a jerk.

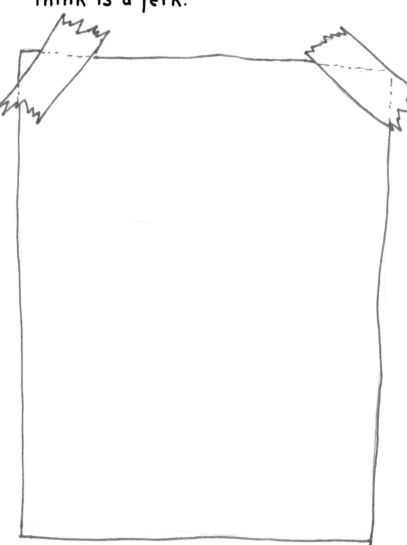

COLOR
ME
BAD

Design or write **the most idiotic decorative thing** to hang on a wall.

Color the **half-empty glasses.**

color.

Write or draw and color
the most irritating slogan.

Draw and write greetings from
disaster holidays!

Name the circles and color the diagram.

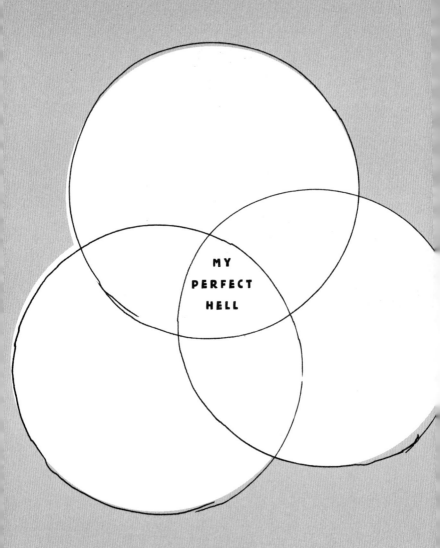

MY
PERFECT
HELL

FORECAST
IS
DISMAL

I HATE

- ☐ Public transportation
- ☐ Drivers
- ☐ Pedestrians
- ☐ Bikers
- ☐ _____

BECAUSE_____

_____

I HATE

- ☐ Spring
- ☐ Summer
- ☐ Fall
- ☐ Winter
- ☐ _____

BECAUSE_____

_____

I HATE

- ☐ Ski jumping
- ☐ Ice hockey
- ☐ Football
- ☐ Javelin throwing
- ☐ _____

BECAUSE_____

_____

I HATE

- ☐ Christmas
- ☐ Fourth of July
- ☐ Valentine's Day
- ☐ Easter
- ☐ _____

BECAUSE_____

_____

I HATE

- ☐ Buying clothes
- ☐ Buying shoes
- ☐ Buying cars
- ☐ Buying computers
- ☐ _____

BECAUSE_____

_____

I HATE

- ☐ Dogs
- ☐ Cats
- ☐ Guinea pigs
- ☐ Pet owners
- ☐ _____

BECAUSE_____

_____

I HATE

- ☐ Heavy metal
- ☐ Rap
- ☐ Country
- ☐ Pop
- ☐ Classical
- ☐ _____

BECAUSE_____

_____

I HATE

- ☐ Soup
- ☐ Fish
- ☐ Pudding
- ☐ Veal
- ☐ ....

BECAUSE ....

....

AT SCHOOL I HATED

- ☐ Art
- ☐ P.E.
- ☐ Math
- ☐ Home economics
- ☐ ....

BECAUSE ....

....

I HATE

- ☐ Leggings
- ☐ Pantyhose
- ☐ Dress shirts
- ☐ Sweats
- ☐ ....

BECAUSE ....

....

I HATE

- ☐ Vacuuming
- ☐ Cleaning dishes
- ☐ Washing windows
- ☐ Ironing
- ☐ ....

BECAUSE ....

....

I HATE

- ☐ Plumbing
- ☐ Yard work
- ☐ Community meetings
- ☐ Neighbors
- ☐ ....

BECAUSE ....

....

I HATE

- ☐ ....
- ☐ ....
- ☐ ....
- ☐ ....
- ☐ ....

BECAUSE ....

....

Have a bad day!